FUN WITH ARCHITECTURE

BY
DAVID EISEN

THE METROPOLITAN MUSEUM OF ART
VIKING

NEW YORK

VIKING

First published in 1992 by The Metropolitan Museum of Art, New York, and Viking, a division of Penguin Books USA Inc., 375 Hudson Street, New York, New York 10014, U.S.A. and Penguin Books Canada Ltd., 2801 John Street, Markham, Ontario, Canada L3R 1B4

10 9 8 7 6 5 4 3 2 1

Copyright © 1992 by The Metropolitan Museum of Art
All rights reserved
ISBN 0-87099-645-2 MMA
ISBN 0-670-84684-8 Viking

Produced by the Department of Special Publications,
The Metropolitan Museum of Art
Illustration design by David Eisen
Illustrations and typesetting by Mulavey Studio, Boston
Printed in Hong Kong
Design by Miriam Berman

CONTENTS

INTRODUCTION

We see architecture every day. Houses, schools, stores, factories, barns, and skyscrapers make up the countryside and towns and cities where we live. We often take buildings for granted, not realizing that every one had not only to be built, but also designed. Someone decided where each would be located, how it would be built, what materials would be used, and what it would look like.

This kit can help you understand how these decisions are made. The text will quickly show you how exciting and challenging architecture can be. As you look at the illustrations, all made up of the stamp shapes, you will discover the many ways the elements of architecture—walls, windows, doors, and roofs—can be combined. Most important, you will discover how to look at the buildings around you. Then, using the kit's 35 rubber stamps, you can build your own structures. Soon you will be able to stamp out almost anything, from a simple bungalow to a towering fortress. You'll learn how to add things like trees, fences, clouds, and cars.

As you become increasingly familiar with the buildings that surround you, you will discover that they can tell us about the values of the men and women who built them and the values that we all share. Of course, buildings give us privacy, they protect us from enemies, and they shelter us from the weather. But if all we wanted from buildings were privacy and safe, dry places we would have had no need to build Greek temples or Gothic cathedrals. These buildings (indeed, all buildings) communicate ideas about the people who made them.

With its perfect proportions, its balance, and its repose, a temple communicates stability and rationality. With its soaring vaults and lacy windows, a Gothic cathedral speaks of the importance of the spiritual in medieval life. The strong, heavy battlements of a castle talk about the fear of enemies, and a factory communicates the importance of efficiency.

When we see and walk through a beautiful temple or cathedral, a stunning skyscraper or a magnificent house, the sensations we feel can be almost magical. It is my hope that using this book will make it easier to understand architecture and the particular joys that it can bring.

THE STAMPS
Building Blocks of Architecture

Architecture is like a language. In a written language, letters make words, words make sentences, and sentences make paragraphs. If they are thoughtfully arranged, they communicate ideas.

Architecture works in a similar way. Small elements are combined to make parts of a building like walls and roofs. These parts are then combined to make a whole building, which communicates in its own way. This is the language of architecture.

The stamps in this kit are the equivalent of letters and words. They are the architectural building blocks that make up buildings. You will easily recognize some of them as pieces of buildings. Others will look like simple geometrical shapes.

HOUSES
This stamp ■ is a complete building. It is very simple, but it has the basic elements that most houses have: walls, a door, windows, and a roof.

This stamp 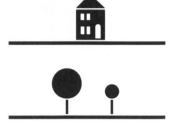 can be combined with a triangle
▲ to make a larger house.

To make trees, stamp a circle on top of a long,
thin rectangle. You can make large trees or
small ones.

With these stamps you can construct an entire
neighborhood. Put the larger houses in front
and the smaller ones off in the distance. Using a
pencil or pen, you can draw the ground beneath
the buildings or a hill in the background. You
can even stamp out a car to make the neighborhood look more interesting.

WALLS
These stamps are used to build walls. The first is solid. The rest have windows.

Rectangular walls with rectangular windows are basic building elements throughout the world. (Other types of walls and windows exist, but they are not as common.) On the inside front cover of this kit and in the following pages you will see some of the many ways that these stamps can be used. But don't stop there. Use your imagination to see what else the stamps can do.

ENTRIES AND ARCHES
These stamps are walls, too. The openings are so large, however, that there is more space than wall. Use these stamps to make entries into buildings and to create large windows.

COLUMNS, BEAMS, AND FRAMES

These long, thin stamps have many uses. The first is a column. The others can be used as columns or beams. The very thin stamps can make frames like you see in steel bridges or in the metal and glass walls of modern skyscrapers.

Here are a few examples of how these stamps can be used.

With the same pieces, you can also stamp out a wall or a cornice. A cornice is the thin band that completes the top of a wall.

ROOFS

These triangles make good roofs.

Not all roofs are triangular, but many are, since this sloped shape sheds water easily. On the inside front cover of this kit and throughout this book you will see ways to use these shapes as roofs, both alone and combined with other elements.

EXPERIMENTING WITH THE STAMPS

Most of the shapes in this kit can be used in many ways besides the ones talked about so far. Triangles can make rounded domes, and rectangles can be used for roofs. (See the chart on the inside cover of this kit for some examples.) It's important to understand how shapes and forms are most often used, but it's also fun to be creative, finding new ways to use the stamps in developing your own architectural language.

STAMPING TIPS
Making a Good Impression

You can space the stamps slightly apart from one another as they are shown in this book. If you prefer, stamp out the building elements so they touch or overlap. This will make your buildings look more solid. Try stamping out buildings both ways.

To help keep your building projects level, you can begin by drawing a line to indicate the ground. If you are stamping out a skyscraper or any other tall building, you can draw very light vertical guidelines as well. For best results, use a ruler. Or stamp out your designs on graph paper.

Most of the time, you will want to ink a stamp each time you use it so that the impression will be dark. However, if you are creating a building or a building element that is in the background, you may want it to be lighter to suggest distance. After inking the stamp, stamp it on a piece of scrap paper first, then print it on your drawing.

THE ELEMENTS OF ARCHITECTURE
From the Ground Up

The building process begins with a design and the selection of a site. Buildings must be secured into the earth. Blocks of stone or poured concrete form a foundation on which the rest of the building can be constructed. If a hillside site is chosen, the foundation must form a flat place on which to build.

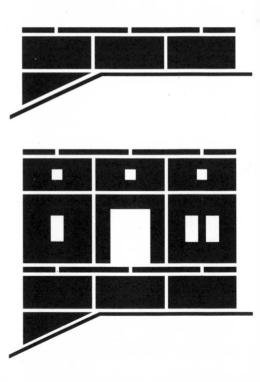

Next, walls are erected on the foundation with openings for doors and windows.

Doors and windows don't have to be square or rectangular. Sometimes they can be in the form of a round or pointed arch. At the top of an arch, the stones push tightly toward the center, preventing the arch from falling down. Round arches seem solid and heavy. Pointed arches push upward and seem lighter.

Large openings can be divided into smaller openings with long thin bars. Small openings can make a wall feel very heavy, while a row of large openings can make it feel light and graceful. Symmetrical groupings feel balanced and stable.

13

The openings in a wall can be so big that there is more space than wall. The openings are usually filled with glass. The size, shape, and rhythm of the openings help give a wall its character.

Walls can be made almost entirely of glass with thin metal frames. The columns that hold the building up are hidden behind the glass. The simplicity of the lines and the lightness of the materials look very modern.

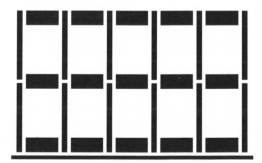

Sometimes a building has columns instead of walls. Beams are laid across the columns. A line of columns is called a colonnade. Colonnades have a different feeling than walls since they don't completely separate the inside of a building from the outside. Colonnades give a building a sense of grace and order.

Classical columns have a tapered profile with a special top called a capital. The proportions of a classical column give it a feeling of elegance and dignity.

Arches can be built across the columns instead of beams. The size and shape of the arches determine the feeling that they give. The spacing of the columns can create different rhythms. One column follows another, close together or far apart, like notes in music.

Columns, arches, and walls can be combined in many different ways. The contrast between a light colonnade and a heavy wall can be very dramatic.

Roofs are erected to keep out rain and snow and sun. They can be flat or pitched. Often they extend beyond the walls of a building. The overhang and the pitch of the roof help give a building its individual character.

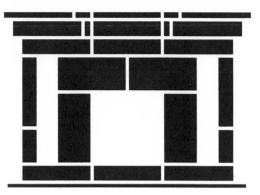

In this building, a triangular element called a pediment tops the columns, walls, and beams. Because it has a low pitch, it seems very stable. A pediment reminds us of the grace and beauty of a Greek temple.

Roofs can even be rounded or domed. Domes are used on many public buildings to signify their importance in the community. It can be awe inspiring to stand inside such a building and look up at the space the dome encloses.

Particular roof shapes are often associated with particular types of buildings. Steep roofs, for example, seem to push upward, and they are often used to top religious buildings.

READY, SET, STAMP!

Here is a fire station. Try stamping it out, then make some changes. Try a flat roof or a very steep one. Use different arch forms and windows that have different shapes. Substitute classical columns for the straight ones on the top of the tower. How do your changes affect the feeling of the building?.

THE LANGUAGE OF ARCHITECTURE
What Buildings Say and How They Say It

Why does a castle look the way it does?

Part of its appearance results from its purpose, which was to protect the people who lived inside. Heavy walls with tiny windows were designed to keep enemies out. Tall towers provided guards with a place to watch the countryside for invaders. Crenellations, as the slotted wall tops are called, gave those defending the castle places to hide. Each part of the castle served a clear function.

A castle also looks the way it does because of the image its builders wanted to convey. The towers, crenellations, and massive walls were designed to look frightening. The spiky profile gave the castle a fierce, forbidding quality. Its builders used the language of architecture to say "beware!"

USING THE LANGUAGE OF ARCHITECTURE

Using the stamps, build your own castle. How frightening can you make it? At the base, use stamps that don't have many windows. Your castle will look strong and rooted to the earth. Above, safe from your enemies, you can make larger openings. Triangular stamps make good flags. Try constructing a building that says "Welcome!" One that says "Stay away!"

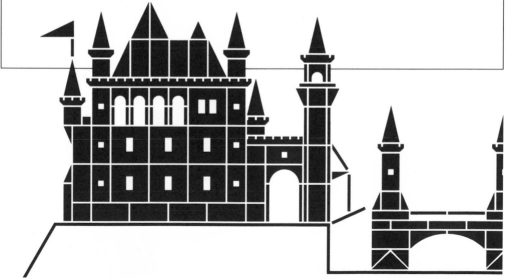

Buildings that do certain things tend to look certain ways. Gambrel roofs, with their steeply slanted sides, are often used on barns. They provide a lot of room inside for storing hay. We are so used to seeing barns with gambrel roofs that just a glimpse of such a roof says "barn" right away.

A farmhouse looks the way it does because its simple form is easy to build and its pitched roof sheds water. The classical column seen here does more than hold up the porch roof. It suggests gracious living and shared traditions. It communicates.

Walls, doors, columns, arches, windows, and roofs are among the basic elements of the building language that help buildings communicate. The overall shape of a building also communicates, helping us figure out what a building does.

A town may have many different buildings that do many different things. Each building may suggest the purpose for which it was designed.

A big building with a steeple and large arched windows is likely to be a church or a meetinghouse. A grand building with a tall colonnade and a pediment is probably an important public structure like a museum, a bank, or a government building. A building with row after row of similar windows is probably an office building, a dormitory, or a hospital with row after row of similar rooms inside.

All languages change over time, and the language of architecture is no exception. Here are three 20th-century buildings. Each has a big, central space. The large windows and the roofs you see bring light into this space.

The architects who designed these buildings used traditional architectural elements, such as columns and arches, but the buildings certainly don't look traditional. The architects used the elements in new ways to express their personal architectural visions and to reflect the changes they saw in the world around them.

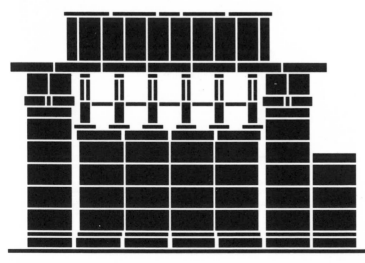

Unity Temple,
Oak Park, Illinois
Frank Lloyd Wright, 1904

First Unitarian Church,
Rochester, New York
Louis Kahn, 1959-67

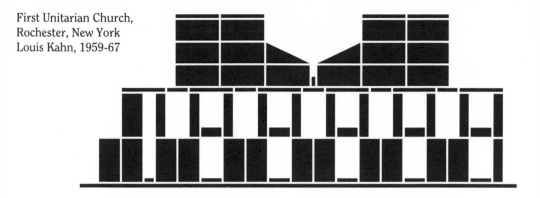

National Farmers Bank,
Owatonna, Minnesota
Louis Sullivan, 1906

These two buildings are in India. One, the Taj Mahal, was built over three hundred years ago. The other, an assembly building, was built about thirty years ago. Although they look very different, they have some things in common.

Taj Mahal, Agra, India
Shah Jehan, 1630-53

Both buildings have distinctive roofs that sit on blocky bases. Both roofs enclose grand interior spaces. Most important, both buildings celebrate something.

The Taj Mahal celebrates the life of a beloved queen. The Assembly Building at Chandigarh, the capital of the Punjab Province, celebrates the birth of a democracy. There are many ways to say "celebration" in the language of architecture.

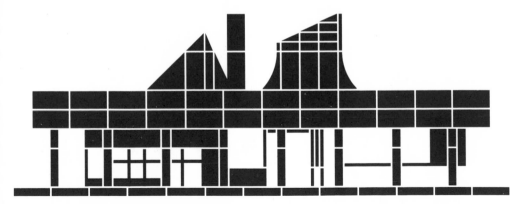

Assembly Building, Chandigarh, India
Le Corbusier, 1964

Great structures such as bridges and factories can also be celebrations. They glorify modern technology. They are designed by engineers who are mostly concerned with how they function and with their strength and durability. Yet the results of their efforts are often works of great beauty and power.

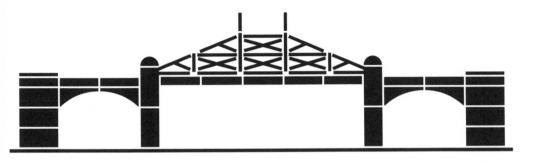

29

HOUSES AND NEIGHBORHOODS
The Places We Call Home

Every building type takes many different forms. We can begin to understand why there is so much variety by looking at the most common building type, the house, and its many variations.

Houses take different forms in different cultures. Space requirements, climate, landscape, materials, and traditions vary from place to place. Some people live in apartment buildings; others live in houses. Some live in cities; others on farms. Needs change from person to person and from country to country.

Yet all houses have some things in common. They protect people from the weather, and they give people privacy. They define a person's or a family's place in the world while connecting them to the world outside.

The simplest house is basically a box, with windows, a door, and a roof. It can be made from brick or stone masonry, or wood. In some cultures houses are made from mud or reeds.

Most houses are more complex. They may have chimneys to let out smoke, steps leading up to the entrance, and a porch. Although a porch is outside, it is still part of the house and connects the private space inside to the public space of the street. In some houses the porch may have two or more columns topped with a pediment. This makes the houses look formal and symmetrical.

A porch can even run across the entire front of a house. The line of tall columns makes this symmetrical house look very grand.

Other elements can be added to the basic house. Projecting bays with large windows let you stay inside and yet be surrounded by views to the outside. Towers can add a dramatic vertical emphasis. Dormers, constructed on the main roof and with their own small roofs and windows, bring light into an attic. Wings and porches can extend in different directions. These elements make a house asymmetrical, and give it a cozy, informal feeling.

Chimneys, bays, entrances, and porches may be combined in many different ways. There can be many different roofs, as we saw in the previous illustration, or everything can be tied together by one big roof.

The houses we have looked at so far have all been very traditional. Early in this century, some architects began to design houses that looked very modern, inspired by ocean liners and airplanes and by new building technologies. Houses like this usually have lots of horizontal windows, flat roofs, and a very light and open feeling.

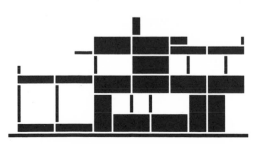

Many houses built since the 1920s have combined the openness of modern architecture with the coziness found in traditional houses. Architects have experimented, using elements from older houses in new ways.

By changing proportions, the pitch of roofs, and the size of the windows, they have made familiar forms seem new. These houses suggest the warmth and comfort we associate with the past as well as the convenience and informality we want today.

34

In Europe most houses are built of brick or stone masonry. Most American houses have a wooden frame covered with brick or wood siding. In Japan, most houses also have a wooden frame, but it is usually left exposed. Panels and sliding doors of paper and wood fit between the columns and beams of the frame. Japanese houses feel very light and open.

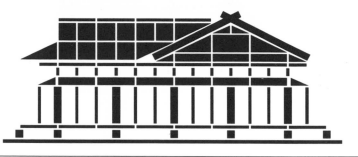

NAME THAT BUILDING

Try stamping out a house you are familiar with. It can be one from your neighborhood or one from a book. The important thing is to capture its feeling. Does it seem to reach up vertically or to stretch out horizontally? Is it tied together by one big roof or is the roof made up of many individual pieces? After you have stamped your rendition, ask a friend to try and identify the building.

The best designed houses rank as works of art embodying great ideas. Frank Lloyd Wright's Robie House, built in 1908, is a good example. Wright used a massive masonry chimney and broad overhanging roofs. They are big and simple and suggest an ancient hearth and shelter. Yet the long rows of windows are like those found on a train or an ocean liner, which were considered modern technology in 1908. Parts of the house are stepped in and out like a natural rock outcropping, while other parts of the house look very precise and machinelike. Wright wanted to evoke memories of the past and connect us to our ancestors and to nature. He also wanted to suggest that science and technology have changed the world and that the future has much to offer us.

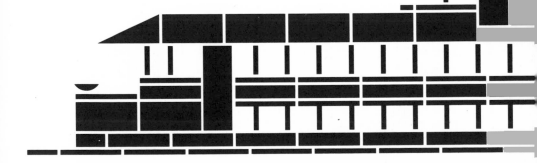

We can use the forms of the past,
Wright suggests in this house, but
we must transform them to reflect
the opportunities life today provides.

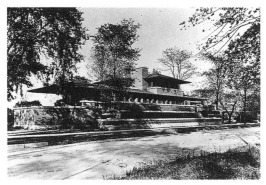

Robie House,
Chicago, Illinois
Frank Lloyd Wright, 1908

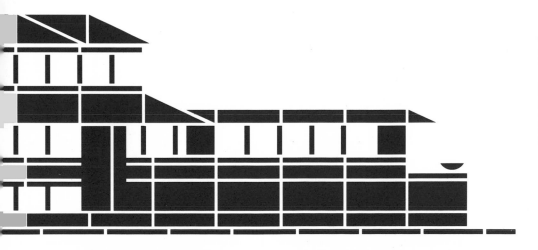

37

Individual houses grouped together form neighborhoods. Houses are tied together by yards and fences, trees and bushes, and sidewalks and streets. The spaces between the houses are almost as important as the houses themselves. People can sit on their own porches or in their yards and still talk to their neighbors.

Neighborhoods look very different in different places. In the Middle East, houses may all be built touching one another to protect them from the weather. Instead of a yard, they may have an open courtyard in the middle of the house. Thick walls with small openings keep out the hot sun.

EXPANDING YOUR HORIZONS

Try stamping out your neighborhood. Are its buildings close together or far apart? Is it made up just of houses or are there other types of buildings, too? Add cars, trees, and fences to suggest the spirit of your neighborhood. For instructions on stamping out trees, turn to pages 7 and 44.

Not everyone lives in freestanding houses. Row houses are tall houses that are built together in a row. They are usually built in cities where limited space makes it necessary for people to live close together.

Other people live in apartment buildings. These buildings are usually large, with one common entrance. People share staircases or elevators, and the individual apartments open off shared hallways. Like freestanding houses, apartment buildings can take many different forms.

In many cities, people live in buildings that have stores on the ground floor and apartments above. Rows of these buildings form urban neighborhoods. Often these buildings extend right up to the sidewalk on both sides of the street. The walls of the buildings seem to shape the space between them. Like a town square or a village green, the enclosed space begins to feel like an outdoor room.

In urban neighborhoods, everything is close by. These neighborhoods can provide security, convenience, and the satisfaction of living in a tightly knit community.

Gehry House (architect's model), Los Angeles, 1985

Architect Frank Gehry's own house, renovated in the 1970s and 1980s, says something about the character of modern life and neighborhoods. Most architects look for order in the world and they try to express that order in their buildings. Gehry's house celebrates the disorder we see in our cities and in life all around us. He started with a traditional suburban house in a 1930s neighborhood. Then he "exploded" it. He cut pieces away and added new pieces to bring in light and make it feel more open. He used ordinary materials like corrugated metal siding, wood framing, and chain link fence in extraordinary ways. The collision of all of these pieces is his picture of what the world is like today.

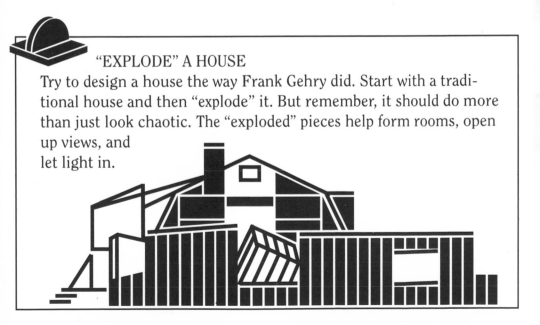

"EXPLODE" A HOUSE
Try to design a house the way Frank Gehry did. Start with a traditional house and then "explode" it. But remember, it should do more than just look chaotic. The "exploded" pieces help form rooms, open up views, and let light in.

SPECIAL EFFECTS
Adding Atmosphere to Architecture

There are many ways to add exciting details and realistic touches to your designs. Here are some.

Try stamping out your designs on colored construction paper. Blue will give the illusion of the sky or water, gray will suggest an overcast day.

Use colored pencils or markers for the sky, the earth, or people.

Add landscaping to your architecture. Groups of trees look more realistic if they overlap a little. To make large trees, use a small stamp. Stamp it over and over again to create the size and shape of the tree you want. Use a long thin rectangle for the trunk and branches. This same technique produces clouds or smoke.

Add gold lightning bolts or stars to an evening sky.

With pencils or crayons, add hills, valleys, and other landscape elements to your drawings. (See pages 56 and 57 for some suggestions.)

Colored ink pads, available at stationery stores, make it easy to stamp green trees, red roofs, brown buildings, or any other colors you want.

Sometimes you may want only part of a stamp to print. For example, you may need to make a semicircle instead of a complete circle. It's easy to do. Put a piece of scrap paper where you <u>don't</u> want the stamp to print. Ink the stamp, then apply it. Finally, remove the scrap paper.

You can easily stamp out many things besides buildings! On the following pages there are examples of trains, boats, spaceships, and helicopters. Use your imagination to create even more.

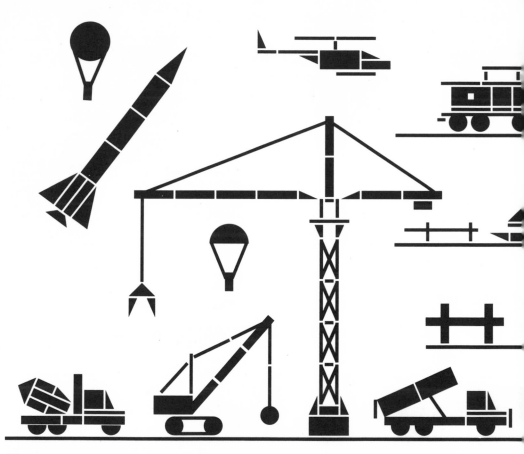

46

SITES
Why We Build Where We Do

People sometimes joke and say that a building is in "the middle of nowhere," but buildings never are. A building is built to fit a particular place, or site, and the area surrounding it. Natural landscapes and urban landscapes both form the settings for new buildings.

Natural landscapes can be awe inspiring. The patterns formed by hills and valleys and rivers and rocks can be reflected in well-designed towns and buildings. An understanding of nature helps people to get what they need to survive: land to farm, water to drink, materials to build with, and a way to protect themselves from their enemies.

Sometimes people must reshape the earth to get what they need from it. If they do so thoughtfully, they can maintain a harmonious balance between man and nature. They respect the beauty of nature while modifying the land to meet their needs.

Like natural landscapes, urban landscapes have an order into which new buildings must fit. A city's structure comes from the patterns of its streets and the forms of its buildings. New buildings should fit into that structure in a harmonious way. At the same time, each new building alters the form and character of the city around it. Cities, like natural landscapes, are always evolving.

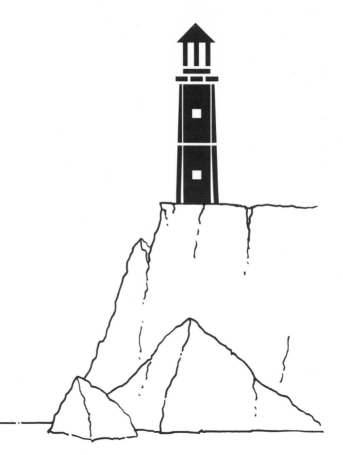

49

HILLTOP TOWNS

Buildings and towns
built on hilltops seem to
claim the surrounding
land. The height helps
protect the people there
from enemies and it
provides a good vantage
point from which to
look out over the coun-
tryside below.

The first building on
this hilltop was the cas-
tle, built for defense.
Over time a town grew
around it. A bridge and
roads connect the town
to the countryside and
to surrounding towns.

51

HARBOR TOWNS

Other buildings and towns focus inward on a central space: a courtyard, a public square, or a harbor. This town is built on a natural harbor, which provides a center for a community of traders and fishermen. The buildings along the shoreline seem to embrace the harbor, giving the town a sense of snug security. Stores and public buildings are right on the waterfront, with houses fitting into the surrounding landscape. Here the natural and the manmade are intertwined in mutual respect.

MODERN CITIES

Most modern cities have
been built on sites that
have easy access to the
outside world. A city on
the waterfront connects
ships to roads and rail-
roads on the shore.
People and goods are
brought together from
all over the world. A col-
lage of jostling buildings
represents many differ-
ent styles and types.

Few traces of the natural
landscape are left here.
Instead, you see a lively
manmade landscape of
buildings and streets.

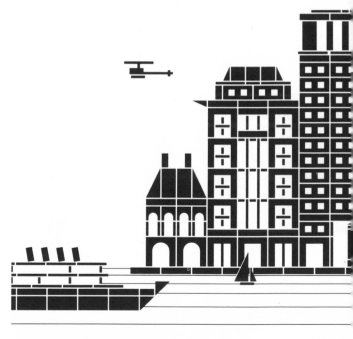

Copy these landscapes onto big pieces of paper (about 11" × 17") or invent your own. Next, stamp out your own buildings and towns complete with trees, boats, cars, and planes.

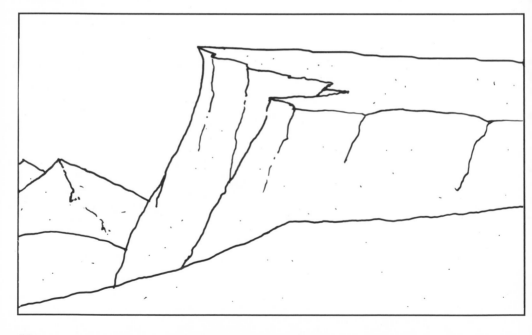

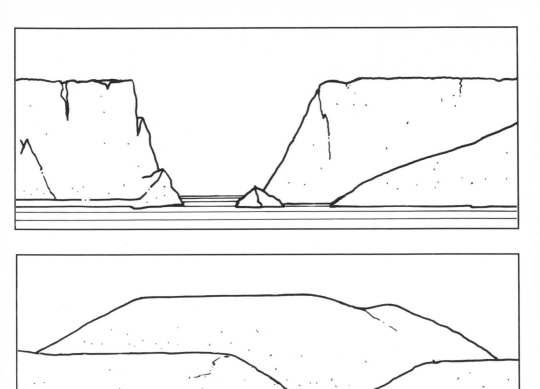

57

ARCHITECTURE THROUGH THE AGES
Megalithic to Modern–and Beyond

Why are buildings from different times and places so different from one another? One reason is that every part of the world has its own climate and landscape, which help determine how buildings look and feel. In addition, every period in history has had access to different building materials and techniques, and both affect the way a building looks. But most of all, every society has its own needs and values, which are reflected in its buildings.

A brief look at changing architectural styles can help us to understand some of the many possible forms buildings can take.

ANCIENT ARCHITECTURE
Many ancient civilizations built stepped stone pyramids called ziggurats. Ziggurats were manmade versions of mountains. In religious ceremonies, priests would climb to the top and perform rituals. The mountainlike form and the rituals gave people a sense of control over the forces of nature.

Mayan Ziggurat, Guatemala, 700 A.D.

THE EGYPTIAN PYRAMIDS

Like ziggurats, the pyramids of ancient Egypt were monumental. They made a symbolic connection between the earth below and the sky above. Complex mazelike passages and hidden chambers ran through the interior.

Pyramid, Giza, Egypt, 2600 B.C.

GREEK ARCHITECTURE

The temples and public buildings the ancient Greeks built did not imitate landscape forms the way ziggurats and pyramids did. Thin, slender columns were modeled after the human figure, and the triangular pediment they so often used was a pure geometric shape. Greek architecture was human in scale and graceful and harmonious. Greek buildings form the basis for what is known today as classical architecture.

Temple of Athena Nike, Athens, Greece
Mnesicles, 424 B.C.

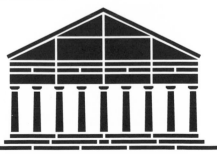

Greek Temple, 500 B.C.

61

THE ROMANS

The Romans adapted Greek architectural forms, but they also invented their own. They developed a building technology that allowed them to construct large buildings for a complex urban society.

Their engineering skills enabled the Romans to construct arches, vaults, and domes, making it possible to span vast, monumental spaces like the interior of the Pantheon.

Pantheon, Rome, 118-128 A.D.

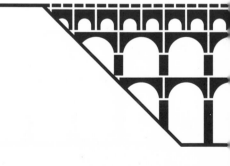

Aqueduct, Roman Empire, 10 A.D.

Among the building types erected by the Romans were triumphal arches, which were constructed to commemorate important events. Processions would march under them into large public spaces called forums.

The Romans also built spectacular aqueducts that carried water long distances, from the mountains to the cities.

Triumphal Arch, Roman Empire, 180 A.D.

Hagia Sophia, Istanbul, Anthemius and Isidorus, 535 A.D.

THE BYZANTINE STYLE

The center of the Roman Empire gradually shifted east to Byzantium, or Constantinople, today's Istanbul. Byzantine architecture adopted Roman domes and arches but used them in new ways. The demands of a different society, with its own beliefs, called for a distinct style.

In the church of Hagia Sophia, spaces flow into one another and domes seem to float above rows of windows. Tall towers, called minarets, were added when the church was converted to an Islamic mosque.

GOTHIC ARCHITECTURE

The cathedral was the most important building in the Middle Ages. Many Gothic cathedrals have large windows and delicate stone carving, making them feel very graceful and lacy. Stained glass fills pointed arches and round rose windows, flooding the interior with light. Spires, towers, pointed arches, and steep roofs seem to push upward toward heaven.

Gothic Cathedral, France, 1200

THE RENAISSANCE

Renaissance means "rebirth," and during the Renaissance architects tried to rediscover the principles of ancient Roman architecture. Using classical elements like columns and arches, they refined building types, such as libraries, palaces, and office buildings. Unlike Gothic buildings, which seem to soar upward, Renaissance buildings seem solid and earthbound.

Renaissance Palazzo, Italy, 1540

ARCHITECTURE MAKES CENTS

Look at the back of a penny or a nickel. The Lincoln Memorial and Monticello are based on Renaissance design principles. Try stamping them out. Now look at the back of a $20.00 bill.

BAROQUE ARCHITECTURE

Although Baroque architecture, like Renaissance architecture, was based on the order and proportions of Roman architecture, it has a more dynamic feeling. Curving walls, light colonnades, and imaginative ornament give Baroque churches and palaces a sense of movement and drama. Baroque interiors are often very complex, with many overlapping spaces that create a feeling of mystery and excitement.

St. Agnese, Rome
Rainaldi and Borromini, 1652

ECLECTICISM

Between the early 1700s and the early 1900s, many different architectural styles were revived. Sometimes a single building would combine two or more different styles. This combination of styles is called eclecticism.

During this period, society was becoming more complex, and buildings needed to be larger and more complex, too. The developing building technology of iron and glass allowed the creation of a new sense of openness.

King's Cross Station, London
Lewis Cubitt, 1850

MODERNISM

The industrial age rejected traditional styles and ornament, and building forms were invented to express a new vision of society. Industrial materials, such as steel and reinforced concrete, reflected the size and function of modern building types like department stores and high-rise office buildings. Structure, construction, and a love of the machine are expressed in many modern buildings.

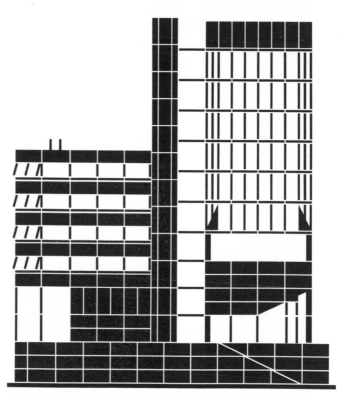

Engineering Building, Leicester University, England
Stirling and Gowan, 1959

CONTEMPORARY ARCHITECTURE

Some contemporary architects invent new forms to reflect the spirit of life today. Other contemporary architects try to capture the spirit of traditional styles with the materials and forms of modern architecture. Steel trusses and large areas of glass may be combined with traditional elements such as masonry colonnades and pediments. These buildings celebrate our modern age while connecting us to our past.

Humana Building, Louisville, Kentucky
Michael Graves, 1982-85

ARCHITECTURE OF THE FUTURE

What will buildings look like in the future? Will they look like the computers and machines that promise to be a big part of our life in years to come? Will they look more like traditional buildings, giving us a way to escape from technology? Or will new architectural forms emerge out of the world of tomorrow?

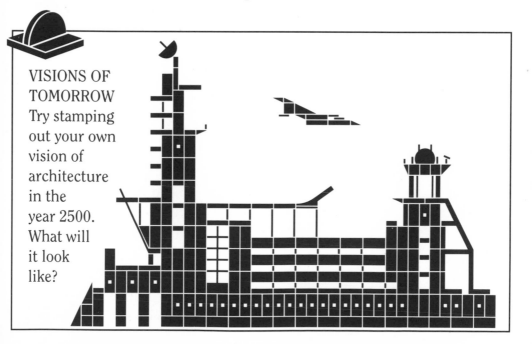

VISIONS OF TOMORROW
Try stamping out your own vision of architecture in the year 2500. What will it look like?

THREE-DIMENSIONAL BUILDINGS
Freestanding Architecture

Using this kit, you can stamp and construct three-dimensional buildings. Start with the models that are reproduced on the following pages. Here's how.

In addition to the stamps, you will need paper or thin cardboard, a scissors, and tape or glue. A ruler will come in handy to draw lines to help you to align the stamped images.

Start with the easiest building, the house on pages 74 and 75. Once you have mastered it, construct the barn and silo on pages 76 and 77. For a real challenge, create a model of the famous Villa Rotunda, designed by the Italian architect Andrea Palladio in around 1522. Full instructions appear on pages 78 through 80.

Begin each model by stamping out the designs. (To make everything fit snugly together, be sure to use the correct stamps and align them carefully!)

Next, as shown in the illustration, draw in the tabs. (The tabs will hold the building together). Now cut out the pieces.

Dotted lines indicate folds. Fold your model, making sure that the stamped sides face out. Then tape or glue the tabs in place.

Chimneys, porches, and other small pieces can be stamped, cut, and assembled separately.

You needn't stop with the three models included in this chapter. You can make three-dimensional versions of other buildings in this book or you can invent your own. Look around your neighborhood to get ideas for your designs.

If you assemble several buildings, you can make an entire town. You can design banks, churches, office buildings, and houses. Lay out streets, squares, and parks. Model cars, trains, and trees will make your town more realistic.

Have fun!

HOUSE

1. Stamp out the house.

2. Draw the tabs.

3. Cut out the house along with the tabs.

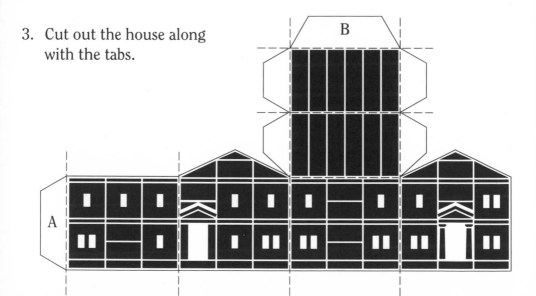

4. Fold along the dotted lines.

5. Tape or glue tab A to secure the walls.

6. Guide the roof into place, then secure tab B with tape or glue.

CHIMNEY

1. If you like, stamp out a chimney, cut it out, fold it, then glue it to the roof.

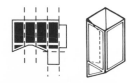

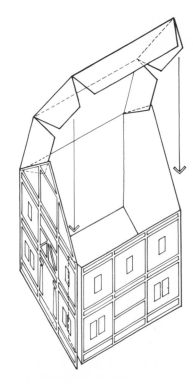

BARN

1. Stamp out the barn.

2. Draw the tabs.

3. Cut out the barn along with the tabs.

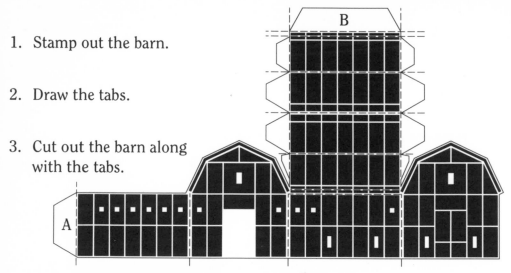

4. Fold along the dotted lines. At both ends of the roof, note that there are two fold lines. Fold them like this:

5. Tape or glue tab A to secure the barn walls. Guide the roof into place, then secure tab B with tape or glue.

76

SILO

1. Stamp out the silo and the silo roof and draw the tabs. (Helpful hint: For the silo roof, first stamp a circle, then stamp small bars all around it. Finally, draw a circle around the bars.) Following the illustration, cut out the roof.

2. Roll the silo to form a tube, then tape or glue tab C to secure it.

3. Bend the roof until the edges meet, then secure the tab with tape or glue.

4. Attach the roof to the silo tabs.

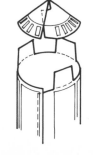

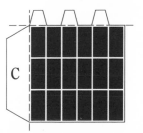

PALLADIO'S VILLA ROTUNDA

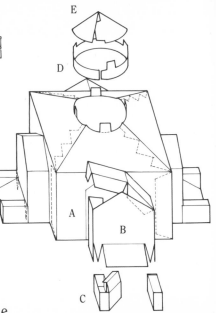

1. Stamp out four wall (A) units and four portico (B) units. Following the illustrations, draw in the tabs. (To save time, stamp out one wall unit and one portico unit, then make three photocopies of each.)

2. Cut out the units along with the tabs.

3. Assemble one portico unit by folding it along the fold lines and then securing the pediment roof to the pediment. Repeat this with the remaining three portico units.

ASSEMBLY DIAGRAM

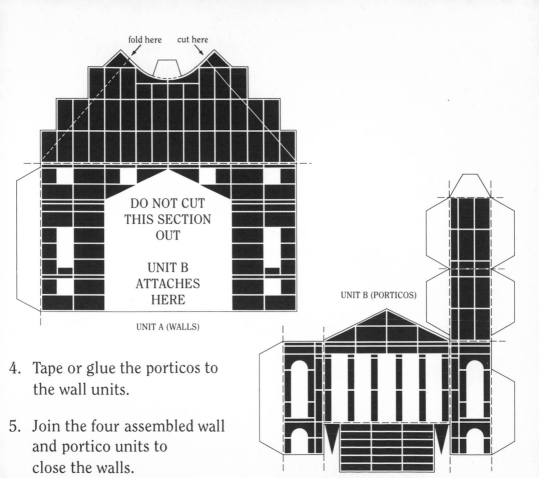

fold here   cut here

DO NOT CUT
THIS SECTION
OUT

UNIT B
ATTACHES
HERE

UNIT A (WALLS)

UNIT B (PORTICOS)

4. Tape or glue the porticos to the wall units.

5. Join the four assembled wall and portico units to close the walls.

(Please turn the page.)

6. Stamp out, draw tabs, and cut out eight stair wall (C) units. These units form the sides of the staircases. Following the diagram, fold each one, and secure with tape or glue. Then slide these units onto the tabs next to the staircases.

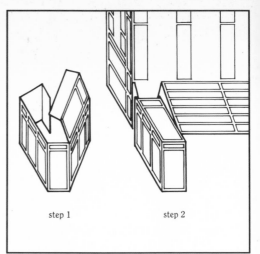

step 1   step 2

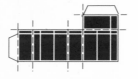

UNIT C (STAIR WALLS)

7. Stamp out the dome support (D) unit and fasten it to the top of the assembled building. (See the assembly diagram on page 78.)

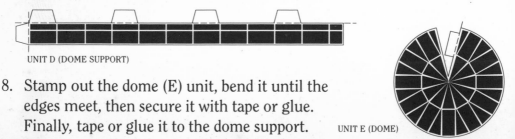

UNIT D (DOME SUPPORT)

8. Stamp out the dome (E) unit, bend it until the edges meet, then secure it with tape or glue. Finally, tape or glue it to the dome support.

UNIT E (DOME)